L. B. Evans working at his favourite hobby

This Love Spoon presented to
Her Gracious Majesty Queen Elizabeth (The Queen Mother)

Foreword

I have given talks and demonstrations about spoons for many years, and have travelled about Wales discussing the lore of the " love spoon." There are many spoon makers, and indeed makers of exceptionally fine spoons, but gradually the makers of the old type of " cawl spoon " and " love spoon " are passing on. Thus the origin of the making of the spoons has been lost in antiquity, but by study of spoons in museums and in private hands, I have tried to place on record my ideas of how they were made, and the pleasure it gives to make them. I have been persuaded by friends and teachers to attempt this work, and am grateful to Mr. Glyn Miller, a prominent member of Bridgend Photographic Society for the photographs of my work. I sincerely hope many original spoons will be made with the aid of this small effort. This indeed will be my reward.

L. B. EVANS, 1971.
Aberkenfig

The Lore of the Love Spoon

The origin of the spoon as a gift to show affection can be sought and found in the histories of many countries.

The Welsh spoon has an association with lovers. While the spoon originally had culinary uses the carving on the handle tells the story of love.

In many countries silver (as well as wooden) spoons were given at christenings with the wish that the recipient would have a fortunate and prosperous life. This gave rise to the saying " he was born with a silver spoon in his mouth "—meaning that the child was born into wealth and success.

I have written this book mainly to help keep alive the art and craft of making spoons, in particular the making of Welsh love spoons which have certain characteristics of their own. The tradition of spoon making has survived for several hundred years.

There are many old spoons in existence, some dating back to the 17th century. The love spoon seems to have developed from the domestic spoon. As the years went by, the handle lost all resemblance to the original domestic spoon, one has only to examine some of the old spoons to learn how this came about. In certain districts love spoons followed a very similar pattern, this was due to the lack of communication in the large rural area that was Wales, each " spooner " copied what he saw locally. Where there was communication over larger areas a greater variation of decoration and carving was found.

The term " spooning " used about courting couples arose from the making and giving of the love spoon. One can easily visualise the country folk sitting around the large fires on winter evenings the men whittling away at domestic spoons and the young man's fancy turning to love. He would then decorate the handle of the spoon with love tokens and probably initials—his own and those of the maid of his choice. If the young woman accepted the gift it was regarded as a betrothal token.

The background of the rural craftsman of the 17th, 18th and 19th centuries is very interesting. The large country houses and estates had their own group of craftsmen to carry out building, house repairs and renovations, the making and repairing of harness, wheelwrighting and the smithing necessary to keep farm vehicles and carriages in running order. Sometimes men followed a few of the trades as individuals. One man could do the required wheelwright's work as well as smithing—this would depend on the size of the estate but it is true that these men improvised far more than they would have in this machine age. Much of this improvisation, patience, craftsmanship and ingenuity was reflected in the design and decoration of the spoons of the period.

A further influence on some of the beautifully designed and finished spoons could have come from some of the craftsmen who were " imported " to the large country houses to carry out some of the superior work still to be found not only in the houses but the furniture. The carving and finish could have been done only with craftsmen's tools and experience—the timber used too was more exotic and the finished spoon sometimes polished.

The decoration and shaping of the love spoons handle is intriguing. The " links " on the spoon are said to link the lives of the giver and his maid together, they also represent loyalty to one another. The " shackle " represents being joined together for life, a " Jacobean twist," entwined together while the " seeds or balls " represent either safe keeping or the number of children wished for the couple. There is a story told of gamekeepers carving balls in walking sticks so that when the balls clicked together poachers would think that a few gamekeepers were approaching and would beat a hasty retreat.

Decorations are too numerous to mention and they are mostly self explanatory. Hearts, locks, keys, lovers' knots, dragons, ships and anchors are a few of the motifs. Inlay of coloured wax was sometimes used as well as decoration by means of a hot iron. Crosses and dates of birth were used on christening spoons as well as on love spoons. Initials, names and simple types of chip carving done with a knife are also found on spoons. A matting tool made from a nail or the end of a piece of metal was used to give a background to some carving.

The traditional loving spoon has something which has all the charm necessary to captivate the ladies so it is hoped that the following description of spoon making will encourage some to follow the tradition of making them.

The timber used in making the spoons shown in the illustrations is mainly sycamore. It can be used quite fresh, does not show a tendency to shake when drying and is easily worked. The domestic spoon when finished may be boiled in water to get rid of any sap and rubbed with salt to harden and whiten it.

Essential Implements

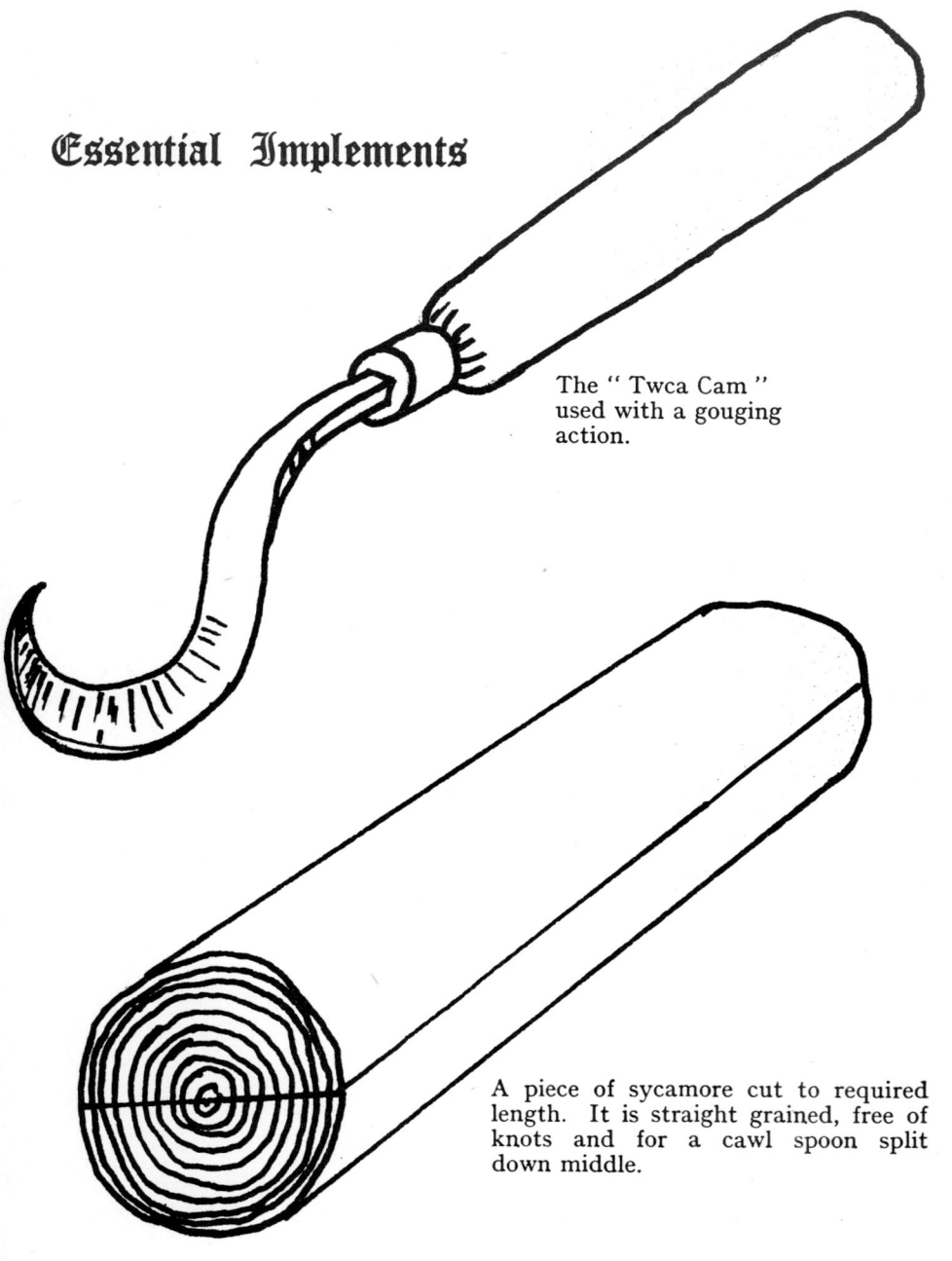

The "Twca Cam" used with a gouging action.

A piece of sycamore cut to required length. It is straight grained, free of knots and for a cawl spoon split down middle.

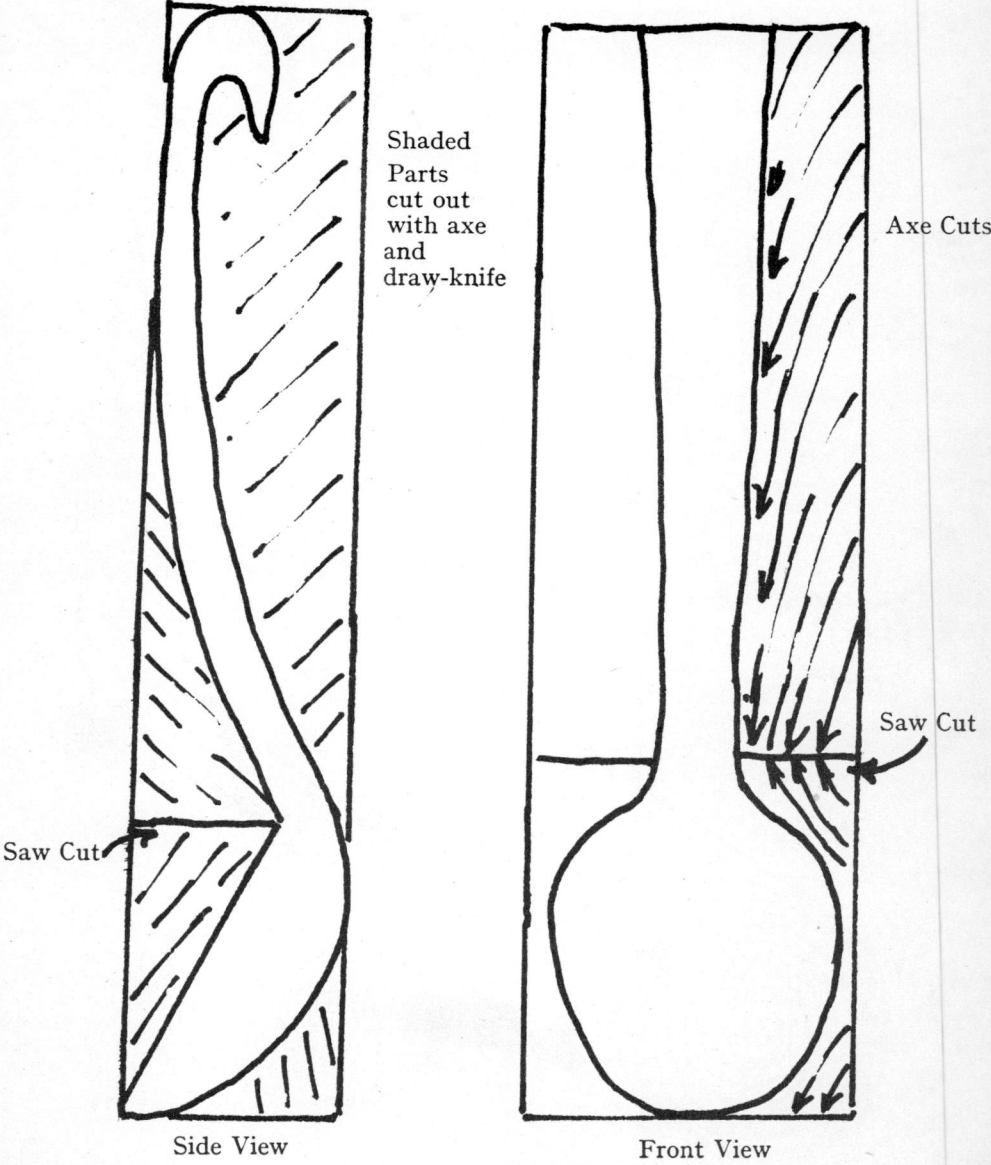

Cawl Spoons

The finished domestic spoon can now be boiled, rubbed with salt, and then scraped with a piece of glass and glasspapered.

These spoons are still used. Unlike metal spoons they do not burn the lips when conveying hot cawl to the mouth.

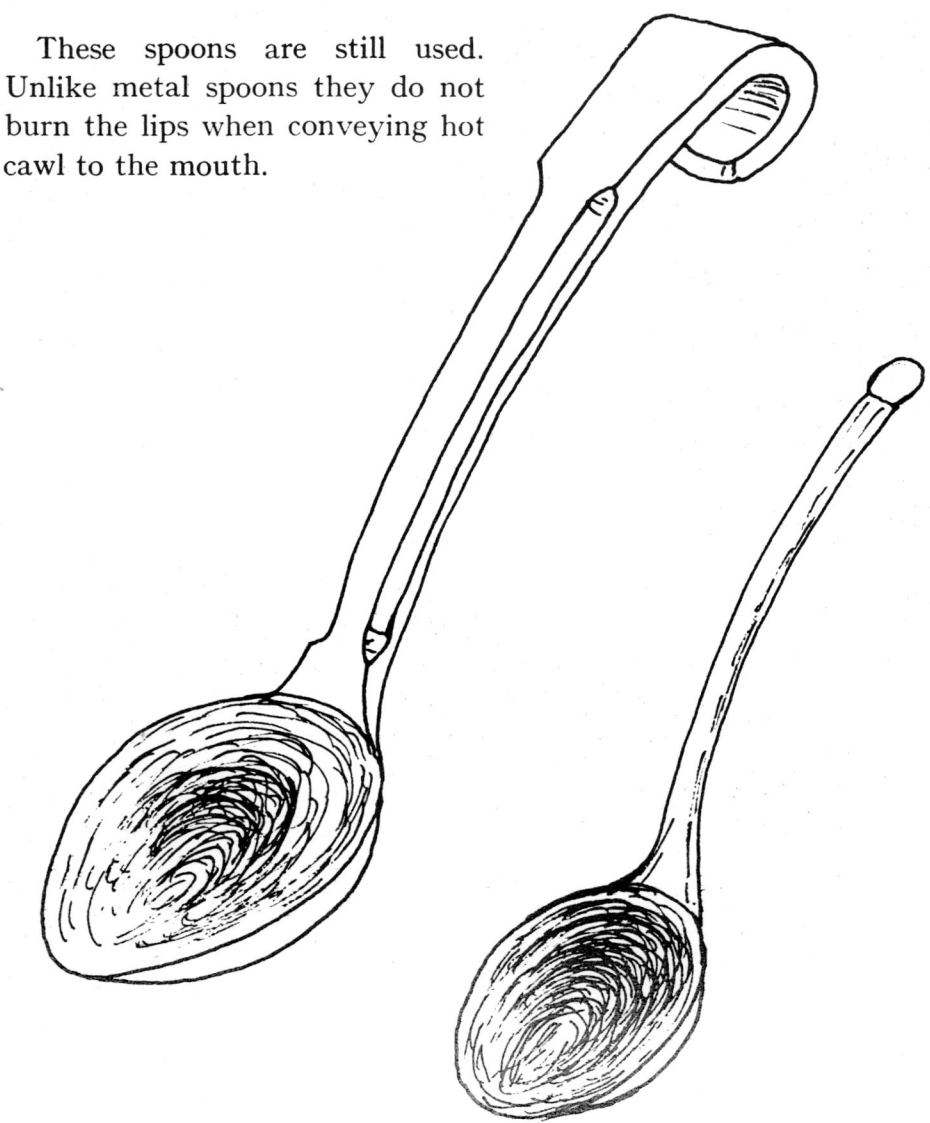

Simple Handle Shaping
showing development of Love Spoon

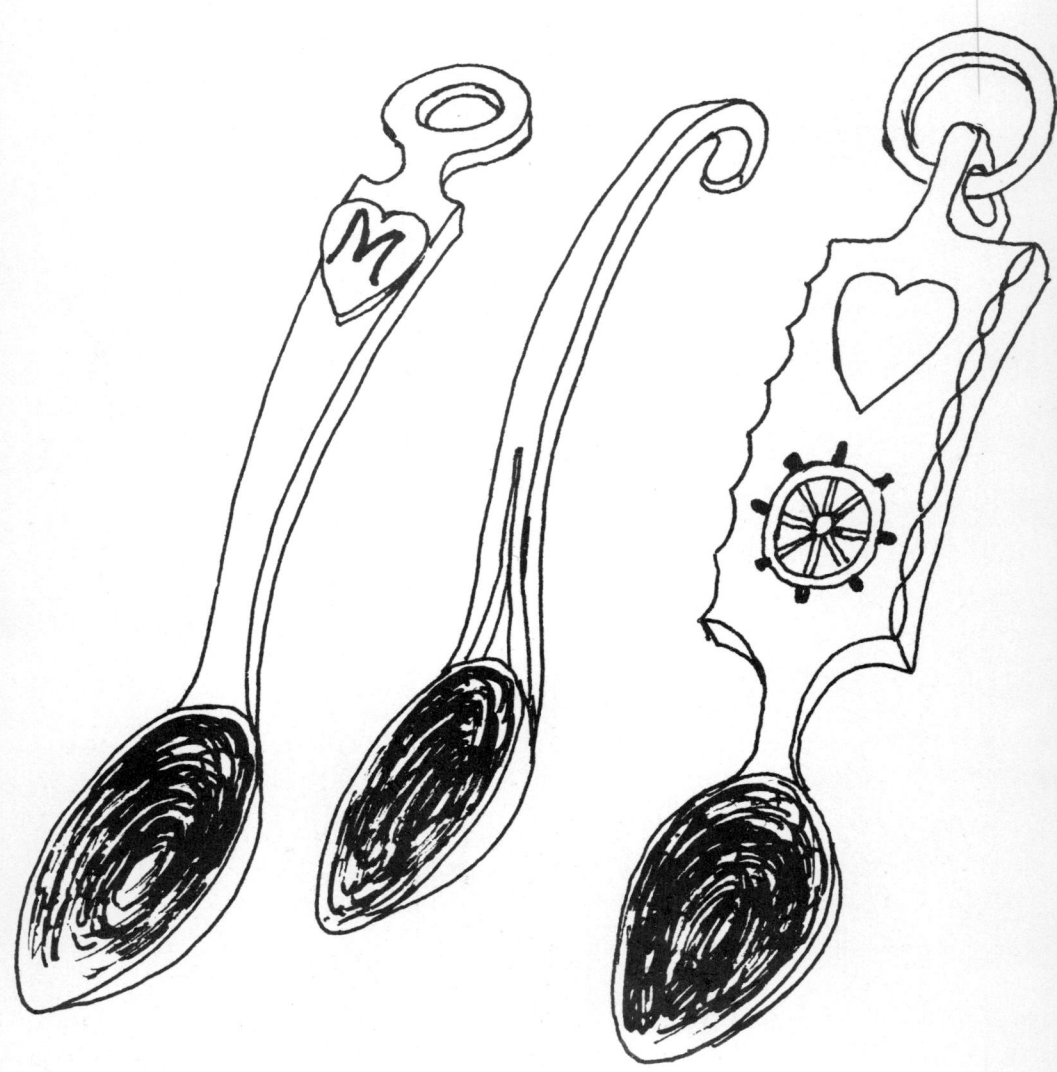

The "Cawl" Spoon
Showing gradual development of the " Love " Spoon.

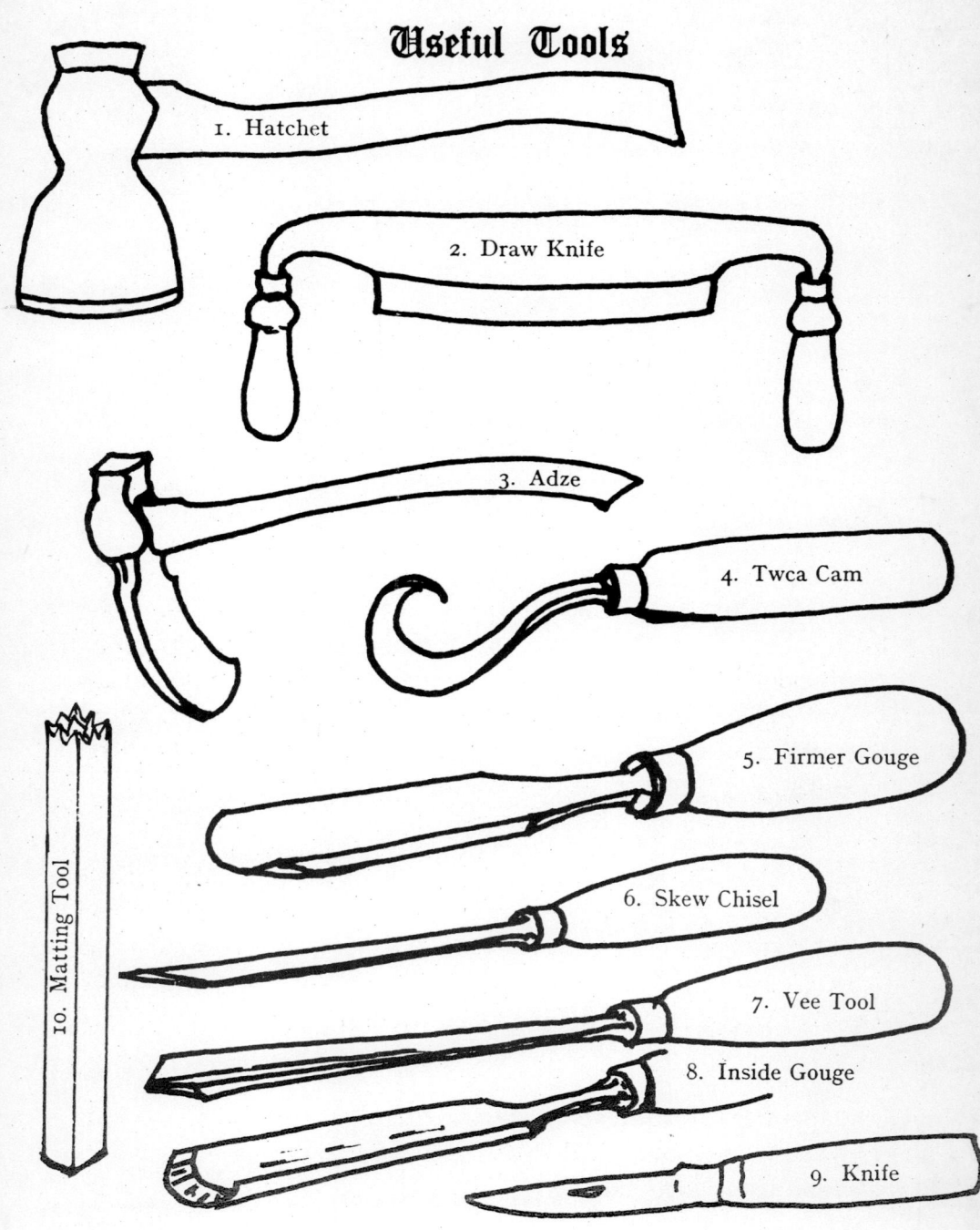

The making of a Cawl Spoon

The "cawl" spoon for stirring and serving Welsh broth was a large spoon made from the wood of the sycamore or birch tree. A piece of sycamore bole or branch, free from knots is selected according to the size of spoon required. It is split down the middle with a cold chisel. The flat surface may then be planed or draw knifed to an even surface.

So that the spoon may be symmetrically drawn a piece of paper the required size is folded in half longways. One half of the spoon is drawn on the outside edge of the paper and cut out with a scissors. The paper is opened out and marked on the wood as shown.

A sharp axe or hatchet is essential for roughly shaping the spoon and having roughly shaped it the bowl is now smoothed with draw knife and spoke shaved. The hollowing of the bowl can be done with a gouge or "twca cam" (a curved knife). This curved knife was used on all traditional spoons and gives a smoother finish to the bowl than a gouge.

The making of the love spoon is basically the same as that of the domestic spoon except that attention is given to the decoration of the handle and no boiling of the finished spoon is necessary. The handle may lose all resemblance to that of a domestic spoon due to the requirements of the maker when carving the love token.

The "spooner" would carve intricate designs and motifs on his spoon to show his young lady how clever he was and how useful he would be around the house.

The making of the Loving Spoons

It should be understood that only one true love spoon is given to the young lady, any spoons given after that mark special occasions or friendships. They should never be sold, but freely given.

The methods used for shaping some handles of " love spoons " are given on following pages. It is suggested that originality of motif be used in decoration so that the spoon becomes a personal gift understood by the " spooner " and his maid.

It is best to start with the simple shape, concentrate on the spoon shape, ever remembering that if a heart is the motif it should be a full heart as shown in the sketch. The best method of getting a symmetrical shape is by folding a piece of paper in half and making your drawing on a half sheet. Cut out with a scissors and draw round the resultant shape on the wood.

The main influence when using motifs for decorations is to relate them to the personal life of the recipient. There must be a happy, light-heartedness about the work, reflecting the mood of the time of presentation. Apart from the spoon, make your own shapes and carve the handle as the mood takes you. In this way you will achieve orignaility and make something which expresses your own personality.

The Shepherd's Crook

The examples on the left show method of marking out ready for cutting.

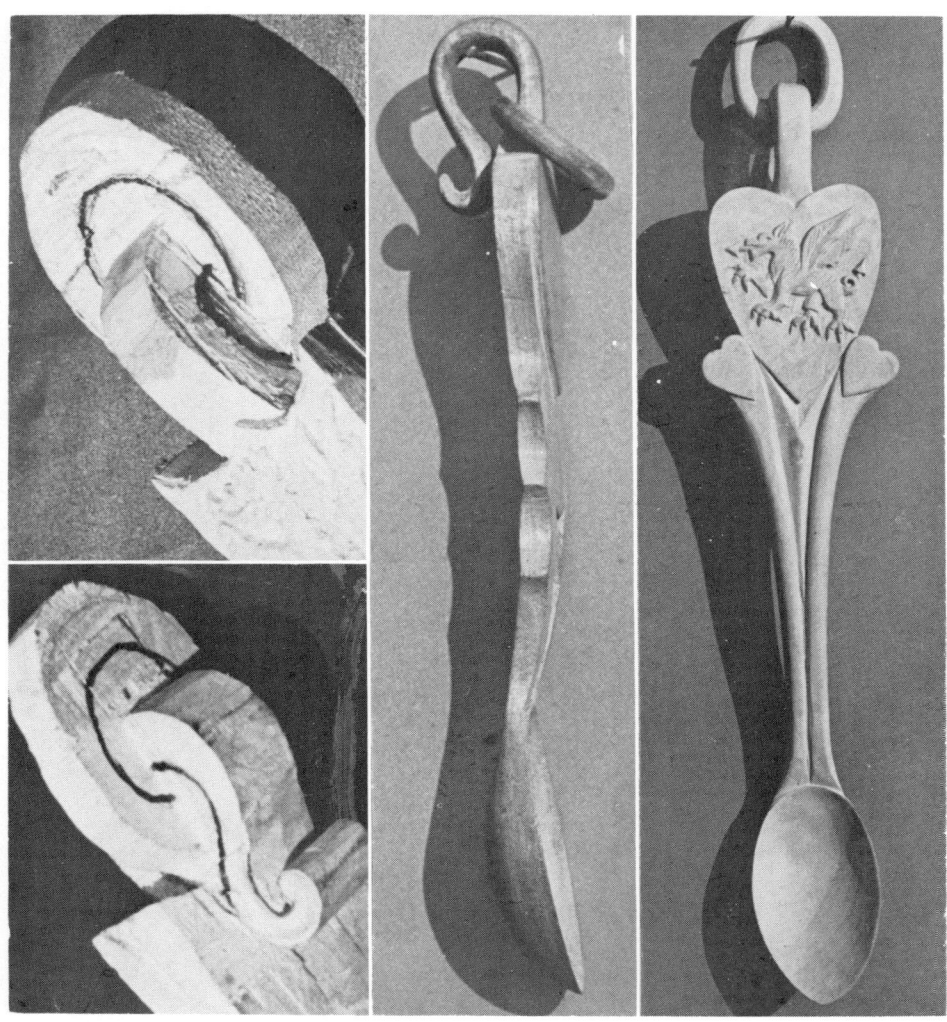

Links for Loyalty

The three stages in making links. In Stage 1. The shaded parts are sawn and chiselled away. In Stage 2 the shaded parts are cut away with a coping saw or fretsaw. In Stage 3 the links are separated with a thin bladed knife.

The Shackle

Three Stages in the process of making a shackle.

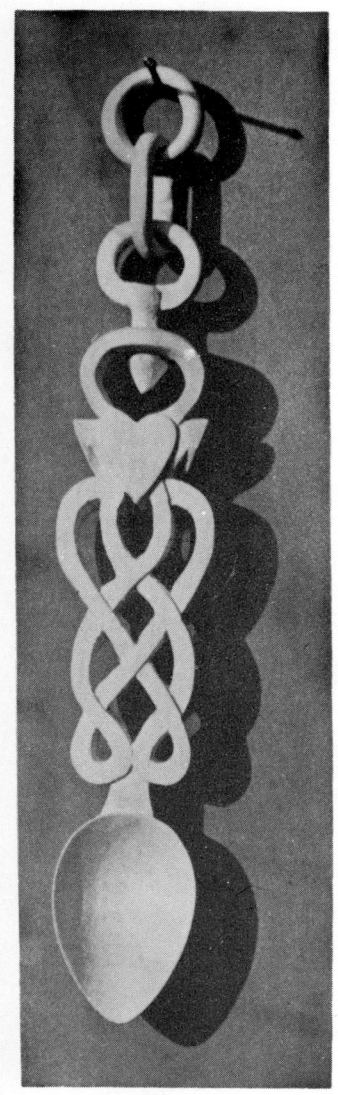

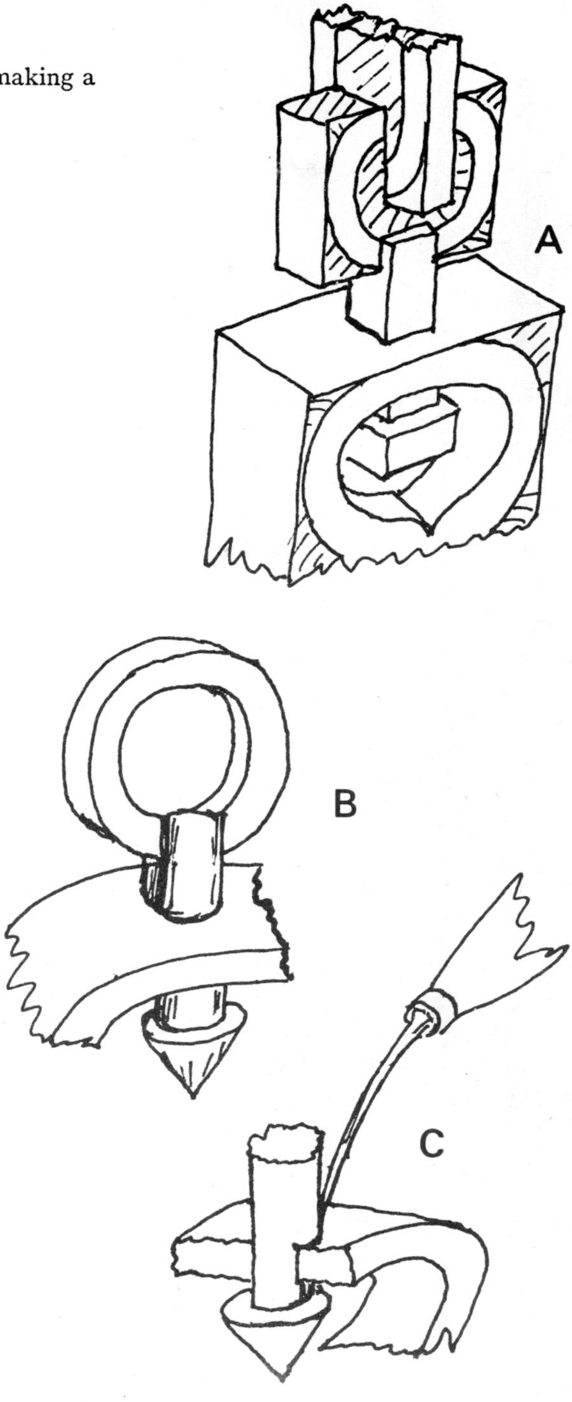

A

B

C

The Twist

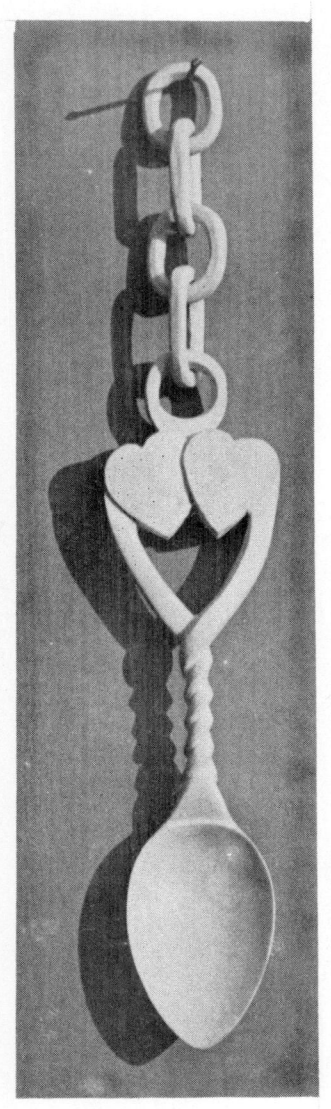
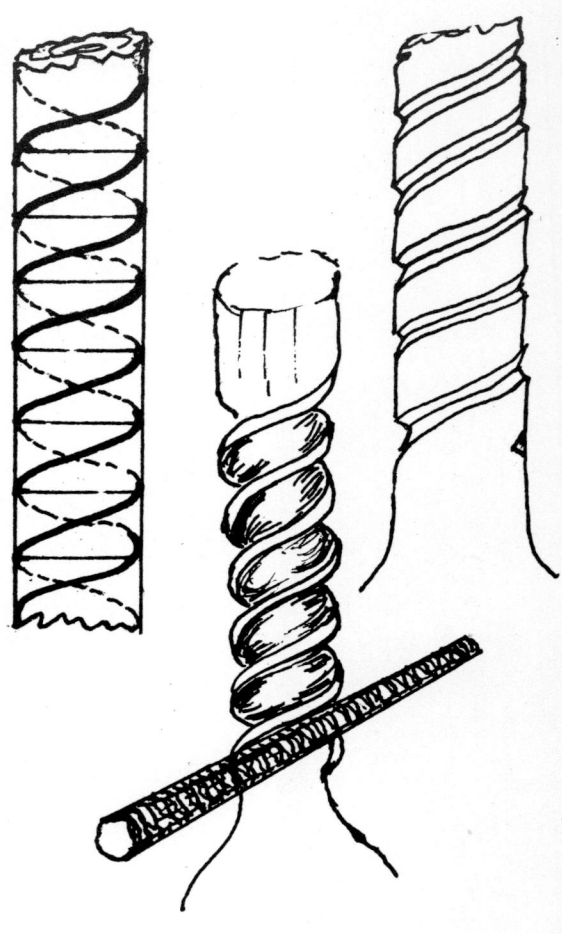

The setting out is shown in Stage 1. It is a double spiral. After being sawn along the lines by rotating the spoon and sawing at an angle. A vee cut is made in these saw cuts, and then by holding a round file at an angle as shown, the spiral is made by rotating **the spoon as the groove is filed out.**

Seeds or Balls

Two methods are shown, the handle is is marked out with the number of seeds required.

1st Method

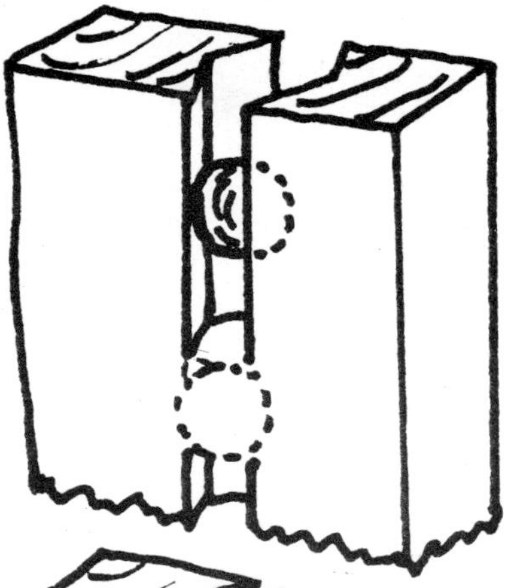

Half Section showing shaping of seeds and socket.

2nd Method

Section Showing half ball and showing portion of ball cut away.

Chains, Shackle and Seeds

These are simple to make. Care alone is needed to cut them out by following instructions. A sharp penknife or skew chisel is useful for this purpose.

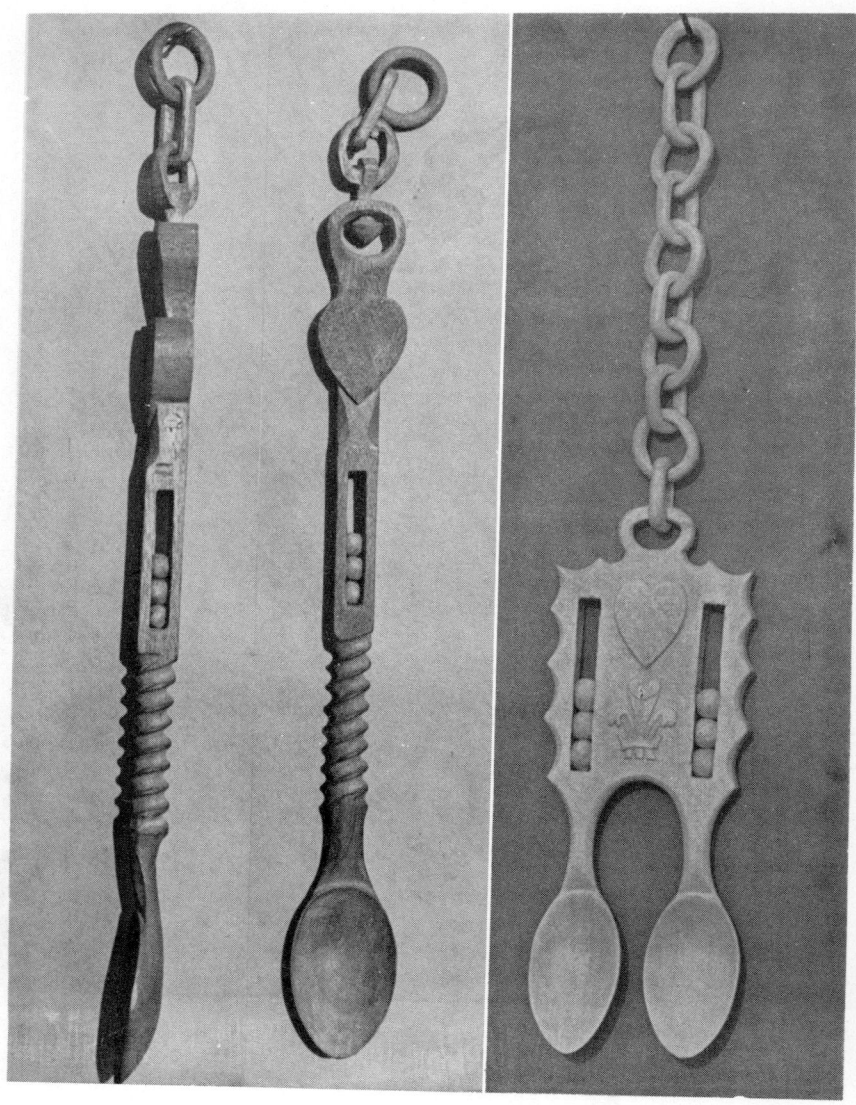

Motifs and Decorations

Motifs give spoons character and originality. Some give wishes, endearments, charms and mark special occasions.

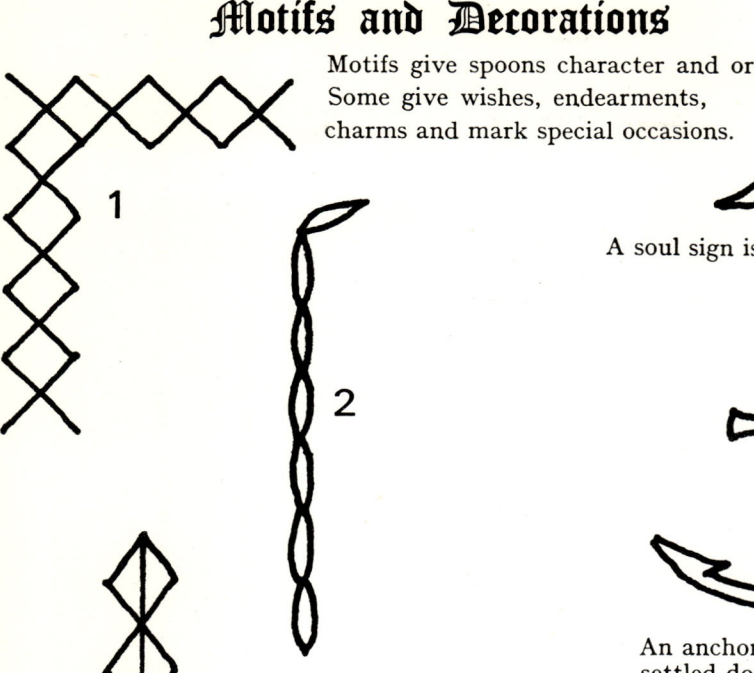

A soul sign is one of affection.

An anchor a wish to remain settled down.

The ship a wish for a smooth voyage in life.

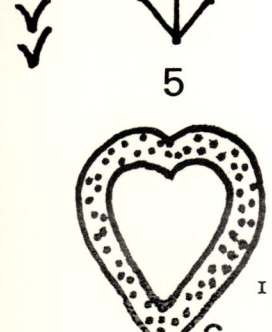

1 to 5 decoration by chip carving
6 use of matting tool.

Circle or wheel of life.

Further Examples
showing decoration suitable for special occasions.